ESSENTIAL POETS SERIES 149

Canada Council for the Arts Conseil des Arts du Canada

ONTARIO ARTS COUNCIL
CONSEIL DES ARTS DE L'ONTARIO

Guernica Editions Inc. acknowledges the support of the Canada Council for the Arts.
Guernica Editions Inc. acknowledges the support of the Ontario Arts Council.

JULIE ROORDA

COURAGE UNDERGROUND

For Gay,
with love,
Julie Roorda
Nov. 15, 2006

GUERNICA
TORONTO — BUFFALO — CHICAGO — LANCASTER (U.K.)
2006

FOR MY PARENTS

Antonio D'Alfonso, editor
Guernica Editions Inc.
P.O. Box 117, Station P, Toronto (ON), Canada M5S 2S6
2250 Military Road, Tonawanda, N.Y. 14150-6000 U.S.A.

Distributors:
University of Toronto Press Distribution,
5201 Dufferin Street, Toronto (ON), Canada M3H 5T8
Gazelle Book Services, White Cross Mills, High Town,
Lancaster LA1 4XS U.K.
Independent Publishers Group,
814 N. Franklin Street, Chicago, Il. 60610 U.S.A.

First edition.
Printed in Canada.

Legal Deposit – Fourth Quarter
National Library of Canada
Library of Congress Catalog Card Number: 2006929266
Library and Archives Canada Cataloguing in Publication
Roorda, Julie
Courage underground / Julie Roorda.
(Essential poets series ; 149)
Poems.
ISBN 1-55071-245-4
I. Title. II. Series.
PS8585.O683C69 2006 C811'.6 C2006-903605-5

Contents

Part One: Elegy for a Vital Organ

Part Two: Enter the Bones

Part Three: The Real Meaning of Life

Part Four: Out of Body

PART I

ELEGY FOR A VITAL ORGAN

Daylight Savings

Though Penelope haggled a deal with time,
weaving and unraveling,
a gentle balance which fostered hope
and a lover's unlikely return,

I would propose something more radical:
let's have time flow fully in reverse,
then see how generous we would be!
We would fill the earth
with gifts of gold and precious jewels,
salve each deep-down gouge with oil.
We would filter poison from our waterways
through our own organs
to produce pristine bounty, milk and apples,
for shipment to the country.

I would sell my clothes for pennies to Goodwill
to be bundled off gratis to the poor in spirit.
A stranger at the coffee shop
would slip a wallet into my pocket,
full of photos and business cards
of people I would be sure to meet.
A lover I had never seen before
would throw open my door with a bang,
find me in tears, want to know me.

Ah, there's the crux,
the certainty of beginnings.

All I Ask

All I ask is divine intervention.

A disembodied hand upon the wall,
not just a silent telephone call;
a Flood, not just a flooded basement.
We should never have stopped writing the Bible
or learning new words for miracle.
I want to find a word for your hot hand
beneath my coat on a cold night,
a touch as full of portent
as a mirage above a desert,
the image of the thing that I need most.
That is not to say I would replace
faith in God with faith in you,

though I have wanted you to change me.

I want to conceive of deity
on any level, as in that ditty
we sang to choose the enders
an-gels, de-vils, wit-ches, reb-els,
unction in a skipping rope,
a timely trip-up, the arrangement
of leaves at the bottom of a tea-cup,
that mole between your eyes,
a third pupil. I would try to name its colour,
which is the same as the hue
between indigo and blue tonight
in the cloud-cast ring around the moon.

It would change me if I knew

a new name for intervention
the world in wider spectrum,
the skipping rope turning
and the hand that holds the twisty end.

Organ Trade in a Civilized Country

Although I signed over a kidney as collateral
for your emotional investment,
I did not expect to wake disoriented
and alone in a strange hotel room
with a fresh seam in my side.

I was naive to believe our contract
transcended the literal,
aspiring to the symbolic
– an outmoded concept of civilization.

Morning is not this shoddy room's best light.
I see secretions encrusted on the mucky quilt
as clearly as an infrared camera
in a documentary I once watched
called *Hotels Undercover*.

I realize now what I should have then:
this country's only language is flesh,
every thought and experience organically manifest
and contained, so emotion
can only be exorcised by bloodletting

and civilized or not
the most common side effect
of any exchange is rejection.

But now I must thank you,
for it seems you excised the very pound of flesh
which housed all my romantic delusions.
I am a little lopsided less a kidney,
but finally aware
that I really only needed one.

The Truth about Daughters

Persephone did not eat
seven pomegranate seeds
ingenuously.

She dripped them
through her hands
like a ruby rosary.

What woman does not
count her wounds lingeringly?
She tasted them.

Still, she'll feign innocence
and don a white dress
each spring to emerge.

She'll bask in her mother's
rage at her molesters
and the harbouring world.

And they will pretend
she is not yearning for winter's
long fingernails to sink in

to the skin of her mother's heart,
and peel it back, to bare
granulate, black-red jewels.

The Queen of Hell

The sun hurts Persephone's eyes,
her skin contracts as she is
disgorged amidst the surface lush
which grows and persists,
a water torture: spring
spreads her like an atomizer.
She mourns the clarity of utter
cold, austere beauty,
the million gradations
of black and pale and grey.

"She's feeling sorry for herself,"
they'll say, "wallowing –"
too soft a word
for the cave she inhabits,
her floors of crystalline
stalagmites, how she circles them,
tests their points against her palm
to feel her skin. She could blame him,
call him Satan, Hades, chemistry.
She could join them in the glare,
take a pill and forget
she was ever misled,
even if God said what the snake
told Eve was the truth –
what is truth to happiness?

Because they'll never believe
she loved him,
their disbelief is her abduction.

Spineless

The moral scale of childhood:
would you eat a worm for a hundred bucks?
would you do it to be popular?
would you eat one to save your life?

They gave full consideration to the slime,
none to five squashable hearts
or a lifetime of swallowing dirt.

A daring show of strength
in the one who plucked
a worm from the wet asphalt
to menace the girl with the messy hair,
to press it against her teeth,
then retreat with cowardly squeals,
"She ate it! She ate a worm!"

Flesh raw and rimy to her mouth,
chill shuddering through her frame,
the whole cold world stomping on her grave.

But vulnerability is courage
underground. The moral scale of worms:
they take no prisoners,
clammy, boneless fingers
that weigh the worth of a life.

Geese Walking

"They say geese mate for life,"
the man tells his companion,
as if fidelity is a sign of civilization,
as if fidelity is characteristic of humans.

"They say to keep your lover at your side,
put a goose feather under his pillow,"
the woman replies. She unhooks
her arm from his to stoop and retrieve
one such talisman from the ground.

The geese choose this moment
to cross the boardwalk,
unhurried, ungainly, hissing, necks bobbing
like insouciant teenagers.

It would be easy to imagine
the earthbound, waddling firm-soft forms
aspiring to be human – if only
they had a fluff of ambition in them.

He puts his hand on her back, hers trails
away from her body where the feather
between her fingers considers the wind.
On a gust, she lets it go,

a signal to the grazing geese
who lift off in unison, revealing
sleek bodies, bulk that is nearly all wing!

Seven in all, coalescing into a living arrow,
intent on the lightening eastern sky.

Elegy for a Vital Organ

I did not know I could live
without you. You've been
pulled beating from my chest,

and I'm still here, walking. To whom
have I offered up this gory gift?
If I knew, could I follow,

and forget my body,
let it fall away, oblivious?
But I treasure this sentient gap;

grief depends on a body.
I sleep with arms holding
the visceral hum of your ghost,

where ripped nerve tips
blast signals into the void.
If a tree falls in a forest,

it does hurt. For I see your face
in the grain of its bark,
smell you in the harsh

winds whipping at its leaves,
and feel your breath, chilling
goosebumps at the back of my neck.

Love is what the body forgets,
but this phantom heart remains,
more persistent than a muscled one,

beating, unkeeper of time.

The Guardian Angel of Basement Apartments

Is less an angel
than a guardian moth
whose wing tips brush
my face in the dark
and remain invisible
– no raiment of white,
just camouflage, fluttering
like a loose bandage.

When someone knocks,
it folds itself
into my wardrobe,
to munch tell-tale
holes in my clothes
till I'm alone again.

It lets me out at night,
in winter,
to fall into snow
and behold the black-pearl sky,
swish arms and legs and lashes,
furiously, so that snowflakes will not melt
in my eyes. Then I rise carefully
from the mould

and look back:
snow moth shadows
wherever I go

and I go down
these stairs.

Earwig

Do not seek catharsis
in the moth
who brushes moist skin at peril
of losing fireward momentum.

Look instead to the earwig,
or rather listen
to it burrow through your head
drawn to dark enclosure of flesh,

harmonic convergence
with your ear-drum.

Feel it spit bitter wax, panic
and employ pincers
evolved purely for the petulant task
of getting your attention.

Give it.
That smallest voice
uttered closer than your own
saying *I hear you.*

Gnats

No such thing as gnat singular,
only bodies of gnat,
ninety-eight percent air
as ours are water.

You must step back to see its shape,
the skin of the swarm.
Too late if you've not paid attention
and stepped into its midst,
too busy reflecting
on your own exquisite loneliness,

as if every blink
hasn't consequence.
In this case, one gnat
drowning in your tear duct.

One set of wings, lately of paradise,
never perceived itself separate,
whirlpooled down a perilous
journey of individuation.

What a shock! Mercifully short,
as it will soon expire and absorb
into the soft black back of your sockets.

Somnambulist, you'll resume the dream
of the egoist, swimming against the current
on this eyeball of a globe.

Everything I regret persists in the form of a small animal

There are more skunks in Toronto
than in all of Algonquin Park.
It's the absence of natural predators, save
"humane wildlife removal"
guys in hemp overalls, their cache
of loops and nets and baits,
psychotherapy for the wild kingdom.

I dream I've crawled into their trap, lured
by peanut butter, ravenous, hoping
I'll wake in a van on the way
to the wilds of Whitby; beaming
with ceremony, hemp guys will loosen
the cage door and preside o'er my first foray
into freedom, forgetting. But morning comes

and the cunning things have licked
the trap clean without capture.
Left a cheeky scent. Heady and perennial
as a bad choice in retrospect.
Where are the foxes and coyotes of redemption?
The Arabian perfumes of forgiveness?
Not in this reeking city.

Regrets are bold and shameless creatures.
Maybe I should feed them,
invite them in, apply their admonitions
like something French to throat and wrists,
the most vulnerable bits. Everything
persists in the form of a small animal:
omnipresent, hungry, demanding respect.

Ladybug, Ladybug

Amazing, my persistent belief in a punishing universe! Who to blame, John Calvin or Mother Goose? *Such a hurry to get on your lipstick, you didn't check – did you? – didn't double, triple check.* Caution is not an involuntary muscle. But the unconscious, reliable as an arresting officer. Stove burners, pots, lipstick. Lots. Raisin Rage and Raspberry Rapture. What if Jesus came back and found you like that? In a cinema? On a Sunday? Forget cathartic flights of fancy, the *fearful symmetry* of black polka-dots and all that. Stack it up to infinite justice, Lady, Lady *Bug*. Better fly, before the Inquisitor torches your kids.

June Bugs

I used to hook
their crisp shed skins
to my T-shirt, a proud row
of medals awarded for bravery,
having swallowed squeamishness:
          the knowledge
          of death to small things,
          their gelatinous transformation.

Today a large scab
crowns a burn on my hand,
a purple, advanced badge
of intimacy with compulsion:
          I reach into flame,
          June Bugs sizzle
          in the porch light's lure.

The Memory Game

I used to know that a good-sized scab
will give you status in the class,

and the blood from a knee-cap is almost black.

I used to know the blue ache of snow
on wrists exposed, the veins too cold,

and the pokable bubbles on hot tar roads.

I used to know the unsporting end
of beetles kept in jars too long

and the flutter of guts when a swing descends.

I used to know the resilient wool
of mittens chewed until they froze,

and the twist of the root when a tooth let go.

I used to know why I watched you sleep,
our restless heat and spoiling sweat,

an elixir of years, for our souls to keep.

Your pillow smells like the you I knew;
I will not wash it when you go.

Cicada

Don't condescend
to call my last song tragic;
don't sigh and say
that nature is so extreme.
Hatched in a tree,
I chose the ground
and seventeen years a worm
before I shed
my larval skin and emerged,
for all of a week,
to sing and die.
You thought it was death already
to be unseen and unheard.
You think it's all about wings.
As if I could be as foolish
and proud as your Icarus!
My tragedy? Now that you hear me
you don't listen. Go ahead,
blind, burn us all in the sun.
I sing for my return
to the yin-soaked earth.

PART II

ENTER THE BONES

Seagulls

A silver fish lies on the path
too far from the shore
to have washed up or leapt.
Perhaps it was dropped by that seagull
screaming overhead with what sounds
so intensely like distress, the pathos of suffering
without understanding,
sadness all out of proportion
to the gratuitous death of a fish
or the ruin of one polluted meal.

As if ability to reason
offers consolation,
as if waste is ever warranted,
loss ever gratuitous.
Then it is not so much grief
I have inferred as admonition,
the failure to account
for pain, a calculation blundered
out of the same "power of reason,"

and the seagull's cries remain unfathomable.
It's hovering over the beach now
in a clash of wind that would take a helicopter down,
sharp sight on the waves crashing in,
churning up the deepest
stores of the lake for prey.

Fine Dining

How it heats the back of my throat
to hear you say that I am beautiful.

If I were a cat, I might fix you
in a tolerant gaze, eyes dilated
to perceive the votive night,
the shadows
snarling with other cats.

But my skepticism spills on the table
with the white linen,
grilled calamari, yellow wine,
as you keep our glasses half full,
pulling the bottle from its cooler
to maintain a faultless chill.

Appetized, you switch to red,
bread and thick meat,
rare to rouse your instincts.
You lift a skin-warmed cup to my lips.

Why would I accept these
libations of a faithless lover?

I have only fancied
myself half-goddess, feline
and flattered
by the smoke of burnt offerings

and though you spoon up lime sorbet,
you will not cleanse my palate.

Compost

Fossilized etchings of waterproof lipstick
rim a dried wine glass
forgotten, red-crusted, by the step.

Potato peelings, coffee grounds, orange rinds
and kiwi fur are all that remain,
contained in your deluxe composter.

Odour-control panels, slots in each side to insert
rods of freeze-dried worms, karma workers.
Given the right amount of moisture and warmth,

they'll return to life, to hasten decay.
It's a complicated mechanism
requiring opposable thumbs to unlatch.

Rodents take notes, and hardly wait for my retreat
to conference at the base
and crack this mystery of evolution:

the seeds of regeneration emerge
from discarded skins, not from the skeletons
to which we've pared each other down.

Chicken Feet Soup

I was not expecting the heat,
the savoury fullness
coaxed from scanty flesh.
More than cooking.
Homeopathy.

Unlike the hand of Franklin
discarded in the Arctic,
where a lack of culinary optimism
ensured a frigid death.

How does one come by
the wherewithal to see
in spindle-bones, in shriveled skin,
mere ghosts of feet,
potential for nourishment?

Enter the bones.
Survival is in the marrow,
and life, like chicken feet soup,
a delicacy.

Value

If you really want
to be worth your weight in gold,
you ought to eat more.

Eating Crow

There is nothing more itself
than a crow, encountered
suddenly in a wood,
big as a whittled black swan.
It stood its ground

and stayed silent, unapprised
of our consideration:
that crows,
with their ability to mimic
the human voice, must be
the most intelligent
of birds.

It circled me on foot,
then it flew down my throat,
lodged in my chest
and proceeded to stretch,

poked its beak out, sharpening
the cartilage of my face;
it turned triangles of my feet,
and unfurled black feathers beneath
the thin skin of my wrists.

Now, crow, I want you to know
how highly I think of you –
but how shall I say it –
Caw! Caw! Caw!

Praying Mantis

You looked so crisp and green
you could have been a vegetable.
It was naive of me, I know,
to introduce you to the cat.

When she crunched your body,
it did sound like celery,
I'm sorry.

You are named prophet;
did you not foresee your fate?
Supplicant, did you doubt yourself
so much that you prayed for respite?

You on whose serrated legs
we model our nightmares,
who would rob moths of the light,
suspected even of cannibalism.

Yet that posture of reverence,
tree-like peace, Zen beingness:
carnivorous flower, fierce prey.

I lay my face against the cat's soft bulk –
no contradictions,
no regrets.

Carrier Ants

A procession of ants
carries tiny giblets
across my back step,
a lit stage between the site
of a sacrificed chickadee
and the long grass.

I can't identify the organs
which are dark and glisten
like pebbles smoothed on a beach,
but there must be a heart,
a stomach, a liver,
all the complexity
of a creature usually defined
as a one-hit-wonder
Chick-a-dee-dee-dee-dee!

Isn't this what we all seek?
To explain ourselves,
each embodied passion
unfolded piece by piece:
here is what I love,
here is what I fear,
here is what I can't escape.

Fathoms that in others we're
unable to acknowledge,
so deafened by the roar
of our own innards.

We are left to these
small armies of understanding,
their capacity to carry
a hundred times their own weight.
May you and I be carried off by ants.

Broken-Hearted Looks on Love

The man steps on the streetcar
with apples mountained
in a basket. The woman

squeals, her one hand hooked
into his waistband, the other
clutching a long baguette,

as the streetcar lurches
before they find a seat. They stay
connected down the aisle,

this couple, wearing shorts,
though it has turned chilly,
balancing that impossibility

of just-ripeness,
every glowing curve in place,
a jig of faith.

Absorbed in their high-wire act,
oblivious to spectators,
they are busy, bearing fruit.

But to taste an apple
one must approach its core,
squarely, with a knife,

or in nibbles roundly meeting
the contours of your teeth.
Either way, there is a danger

you will nick the scaly chamber
        of its heart. The couple
                rise together, resume the dance,

pull-string, traffic, steps – intact.

Swan Formation

Winged and floating,
    spanning the lake
        and a bank of white fog,

ghostly possibility of Swan,
    crystallized to a pair,
        parents, and one cygnet.

        Yesterday they had two.

It is their consciousness
    of immortality, which separates
        swan from human,

and the wooden dock
    of Ashbridges Bay.
        Try, try not to look away.

Design

If ever a creature were designed
to lure us into its consciousness,

it is the swan, when its wing elbows open
in promise of enfolding whiteness,

showing us it is possible
to land on water. The cygnet has grown

as big as its parents. Together still
they feed, float, and this morning, flew

in silent triangulation
over the water, tracing the curve

of the inlet to the bay,
necks straightened, like soft darts

against a hard cityscape.
They banked to descend,

on no visible signal, just wings
stroking at last in unison.

Threshold

The swans have come around
	to the open lake, now
		that the bay is frozen over,

the cygnet finally moulted to white,
	like the ice-floes they resemble
		the bowed branches at the edge,

weighted by the onslaught of winter waves.
	As a woman draws her scarf tighter to her mouth,
		frost blooms in the black wool

and the swans swim steadily into white-caps,
	as if they offer no resistance, as if their cycling feet
		and the lake's current complement,

breath-in-breath-out, heart beats.
	It is the privilege of humans
		to ponder past and future,

but it is not the swans who are
	surprised by desperation,
		its frozen-metal kiss.

She seeks the shore for intercession
	– mermaid? tidal wave? reversal of season? –
		averts her face from the answering wind,

and the swans slip around the point
	like satellites, as the pale sun holds
		to the southern horizon.

PART III

THE REAL MEANING OF LIFE

Extinction

In 1901,
in Beresovka, Siberia,
they found an ancient woolly mammoth
frozen upright, with food in its mouth
and fresh buttercups in its stomach.

The beast that is us would be so lucky
to meet an end as sudden,
as if an asteroid had annulled the sun;

an end without the pernicious unraveling
of conversation, tedious as the afternoon
we spent picking gum from my hair;

an end without the creeping disarray
that made us turn our clocks back
a week too early,
forget to eat meals and fail
to notice the cat had contracted worms;

an end without missing pieces
like that one china dish, forgotten
where it collects mud
under the Christmas-blooming cactus;

an end in spring.

After all, the mammoth's decay
may just have been delayed
by two years, or two million,
now that scientists pillage its DNA
and prepare to birth its clone.

Imagine the orphan alone,
its own species, and knowing nothing
in the world but the need
for fresh buttercups.

Caesura

Recently widowed
she finally felt so low
that she severed her left hand
with her late husband's table saw.

Though he'd always raved about the tool's accuracy,
she was surprised to have the opportunity
to observe that the slice
was indeed clean and sharp.

She had expected to lose consciousness
at the moment of separation,

but had not locked the door,
nor accounted for her daughter's
uncanny sense of timing.

Though stretched by years
flesh was still their instrument of intuition,
forged across her uterine wall,
she'd poked back each time a limb
pressed out, a prenatal game
of telephone to allay
the anguish of immobility.
Thus honed, a sixth sense
of body inside body.

Her daughter carried the limb upstairs
and placed it in the freezer
to await the ambulance.

*

The cut-off hand, meanwhile,
had a near-death experience.

It floated above the kitchen
and entered a long, dark sleeve
with a bright light at the end.
That's where it found him,
his face it could read like Braille.
He held it as the touch
of all it had ever been
fleeted along its fingertips,

prick, prick of pins,
little girl learning to quilt,

his back under the sheets, hot as a grill,

the hard drum of a pregnant belly,
the stickiness of kids,

the numb cold,
letting go,
countless gloves and mittens.

It wanted to stay,
but he sent it back
with his wishes.

⋆

Wrists were the surgeon's specialty,
though she'd really wanted to be a filmmaker,
pretended she was splicing frames
together, instead of flesh,
the most delicate of sutures
rejoined muscles, tendons, veins,

and appealing to that very human capacity
to imagine lines and cracks away,
the persistence of vision,
she stitched the skin.

*

Reattached,
the hand determined to show
its widow
what it had known.

It crept away in the night
to gather lilacs for her bedroom.
It wrote her love letters,
and played "I Fall to Pieces"
on the piano.

Early on it had to pinch her
to assure she was awake.
Blood continued to pump
through the repaired veins of her wrist,
and each drop, as it made the trip
came back charged

with expanded intuition
of body inside body
forged across temporal walls

our caesural skin.

The Sculptor in Winter

Sculptures of unmortared
rocks impossibly stacked
appear each morning by the lake,
like ancestors, or amphibious
soldiers mounting the beach.

Today, the windchill minus thirty-four,
one glyph, tall and solitary, an unrequited lover
staring out at the polished-tin sea, in the pale
clarified light of a sun which will rise and set again
in the south. Only the hardiest
dog-walkers gather to appreciate
the Sisyphean drama of form;
knowledge of imminent toppling seasons
their delight. Precariousness and its relishment.

Compelling enough to draw
an anonymous sculptor (lover) to the water's edge
despite, or because of the cold, and these few left
with their plaid-coated dogs,
who wonder silently whether gravity
is the real meaning of life.

The Quality of Darkness

Three a.m., the topic on Radio One
is light pollution.
They trot out fearful statistics:
blind women have fifty-percent less
breast cancer than the seeing;
frogs caught in the nimbus
of football stadium lights refuse to breed.

The radio entreats me to assess
the quality of my darkness:
unplug the microwave's flashing red clock,
stop seeping streetlights with sheets.

My eyes are as my skin, sensitive
as the pervious covering of amphibians,
feeling the press of darkness, being
more than just the absence of light,
in which sight sidles inward,
snowballs, bigger than I thought

I was when I was
defined by light, without which nothing
is separate. I can hear the frogs now,
so close, inside my chest, scraping the edge
of a minor chord and listen!
It's the same old song: *Save me, save me.*

No angel will interrupt
the drone of Radio One.
It's three a.m. The darkness speaks:
do not sleep through this.

Ode on a Lazy Eye

It allows me to be evasive,
wandering with the one,
while the other eye, staring
at your forehead, unnerves
because you do not know
in which window to peer.

But it's not up to you.
I switch at will
from one eye's view
to the other.

Or combine the two perspectives
for a deconstructive image,
the world a Cubist canvas.

Wall-eyes can be claustrophobic,
and the restive straggler
will eventually stray more freakishly off-track
in search of some transcendence.

Where else to go but in?
Eyeball rolling back
to the unfolding inner skull
close-up on the machinations of vision.

You may be alarmed
by this unseemly introspection,
and accuse me of having a fit.

Don't worry,
as long as I eschew the three-dimensional
world produced by two eyes
diverging a mere centimetre,

and exist along
a kaleidoscopic horizon
of infinite vanishing points,
fit is something I'll never do.

Night Blindness

The orange triangles
which line the curves of the road form
not a fence,
                    but an assumption
that if I cast my high beams
steadily and confine
my route to the flat space
between my face and its reflection
I will remain
                      safe.

I should not drive at night
at all,
                    not with my wonky eyes,
sneaking apart
to seek unconfirmed aspects
and nebulous meridians
and generally wreaking havoc
with anything
                      that might be
construed as common knowledge.

My eyes are liable to trick me
into thinking my bulk
                        slim enough to slip
between the blinkering signposts
where I'll push back the cool swats
of umbrageous branches,
and my bare toes will clench holds
  in the grassed mud inclining
              to the edge of an invisible stream.

When I smell its sagey damp,
I'll find I comprehend
the frogs' song lyrics,
and come to believe
  I see more clearly
          in the luscious absence of light.

Closer to Real

Aliens are not convinced
that we exist.

But there are those among them,
who want to believe, who persist
and pursue us to our beds,
to probe for some avenue
through the density
which makes us
most implausible –
the weight of a body,
wet, pulpy biomass.

The disembodied can barely imagine
such sarcophagal casing sustaining life.
The slow suffocation
of feeling on the inside
peeking out!

It's a flimsy illusion that disintegrates
as soon as sleep exalts us
like a popped cork,
sends us spilling over
the lips of the universe

and tips the watchers off.
Sudden erratic patterns
appear on their radar screens that resemble
drunken partiers with flashlights
romping into a woods in the dark.

That's why they come to us at night
when we are closest to real,
when we are dreaming.

The Pros and Cons of Ghosts

I've given birth to a ghost.
It's been a long hysterical pregnancy.
Challenge enough
to bear a child out of wedlock,
so much more to have a child
without benefit of flesh.

No pablum or milk,
she'll suckle my breath;
no voice to cry, her scrutiny
will warn me awake;
she has no comforting weight,
holding her feels like floating away,
flying, just high enough
to clear the rooftops of you, my rivals
in philosophy, with whom I must plead
the advantages of ghosts.

Look, she's learned to fly so fast!
Being a ghost
she won't be required to forget.

A true, devoted parent,
I invest in her all my desires
and live vicariously
as she slips through the cracks
of your locked doors,
runs through your hair
like chilly fingers.

Fine. Insist that she,
whom I love most, does not exist;
you won't detect her stuck-out tongue,
the hopping ghost-frogs snuck into your desk

Slow Letters

I must believe they survived,
   for there they are!

Vital as the man who mounts a rock
   to face Lake Ontario
and Mecca: thin branches newly freed
   from the weight of ice

that encased them barely a month ago,
   greeting the breeze with a palsied
sway that reminds me
   of your wrist

hovering above the alphabet,
   that arrangement which so resembled
one poised at a Ouija board, directing
   with the slightest touch,

slowly letters, finally words.
   I knew some who doubted
and defended with fury
   my faith in you, you speaking

across the hemisphere of your flesh.
   So what of your death?
Shouldn't it be less of a struggle
   to reach me now?

The chorus of two-note duck calls
   on the water seems to me mournful.
It's that which makes us human,
   here, isn't it? That backward glance

unknown to birds and the three-legged
   dog who bumps me mid-
rapturous flight to catch a frisbee.
   "He only grazed me," I assure

an apologetic frisbee-tosser.
   The slightest touch.
I've suddenly realized
   how it is we are alike!

I too can only spell it out:
   how a small collision with ecstatic,
hobbled flesh jolted me,
   speechless; how I'm crawling

now, back to the beach to bow
   down in the gaze of the sun.

Relief

A grey heron wades in the inlet
    by the marina, where a large crane raises
        sailboats from the bay;

beyond, the city's spiky tower
    stands crisp, the dawn light skips
        like a flat stone across the lake.

"*Luna Sea.* Are you ready?"
    A man with a megaphone
        calls boat owners to the dock to witness

the last kiss of water to the hull,
    pronouncing each name solemnly:
        "*Aquaholic.* Please step up."

The heron quilts the filthy shallows
    with its needle-thin legs, below
        the growing line of boats

bedded above the surface of the water
    in a row of wooden bunks.
        "*Mid-Life Crisis.* You're next."

It snags a fish in its chopsticks beak,
    lifts a paper-sharp knee,
        and tests its voice, a deeper squawk

than a seagull's, the same keening key.
    "*Out-of-Body Experience.* Go ahead."
        It waits, till a backdrop of boats

contrasts the steel November sky,
    to rise, on the power of wide wings
        belying that thread-like legs

ever held its weight. It flies,
    in high relief the entire length of white,
        then disappears south.

PART IV

OUT OF BODY

Hereafter

Tonight they transplant to my chest
the heart of a ninety-seven-year-old woman
struck by lightning, climbing a tree.

I watch them put it in,
see it hovering above me
purple bleeding into crimson
with gold piping.
It sizzles some, still charged
with the blast that knocked her
to kingdom come.

I cry to know
why hers is more viable,
why it thrived,
marinating in her chest,
spiced and sweetened,
tenderized by time,
while my own withers away
to a mere grey thread
in only a fraction of her years?

When I awake I will see
she is me,
this suture in time
has granted the living fantasy
of giving back to youth
the expanse of age,
to sleep, lucidity,
to now, hereafter,
meanwhile I'll count the beats
between the lightning
and its thunder.

Joy

When it returns
it will cross serotonin-starved
synapses like a tsunami.

It will sweep with the rush
of a thousand taffeta dresses
rising in a gust.

It will explode
like wasabi through my nose.
Onions will weep in my hands.

It will return to me the eyes
of a prodigal child:
everything will be bigger
than I remember.

The Altruist

1. Justify Yourself

To give is suspect;
to donate half one's liver
doubly so. I must convince you
of my soundness.

You, the psychoanalyst,
adopt a willow-tree posture
of understanding, but I know it's a test.
"Why do you want to do this?" you ask.
You eyes appraising as a cat's.

(Hmmm, what not to say:
that I have a guilty conscience,
am a lapsed Catholic,
lapsed Calvinist,
prelapsarian,
masochist,
Manichean,
Munchausen by proxy
or under the influence of aliens.)

2. Selfishness

My mother cries.
I thought she'd applaud
this prodigal redirection,
but she sees only the risk.

Forever misinterpreting the dynamics of this relationship,
I've inflicted another blow.
Shouldn't you rather have a baby,
if you must do something unselfish?

I dream of rare cooked liver
trussed with a bonnet
laid in a pram.

Don't come searching for me,
Kiddo, when you're eighteen.
You'll find me lacking.

3. No Essay Questions

Sterile halls,
walls wiped of trailing fingerprints, stretcher-level smudges.
Floors Zambonied antiseptic.
Battery of blood drawn, breaths measured,
body probed and tallied.
This is unambiguous:
        true or false, multiple choice.
        One right answer.

How did it happen?
Corporeal primacy,
physicians as clergy
mediating what's little left of the divine:

        the raw worth of a pound of flesh
        (as opposed to, say, a poem.)

4. Accounting for Poets

Prowling for my motive,
you say, "I'm worried
about your Self-Esteem."

What, when the world
warrants I'm not pulling my own weight?
I'll be lighter minus
two-and-a-half pounds of liver / guilt,

and I've figured the way to tabulate one's worth is this:
imagine you're dead, alone in your apartment.

Count the phone messages
        left warning
        your books are overdue.

Subtract the weeks it takes your boss
        to fire you.

Multiply the percentage
        of your body mass consumed by cats
before the hearse arrives. Then add

the lengths to which your mother will go
to stop you.

5. Synchronicity

Mom has begun a prayer chain,
an email circle of church-going friends,
asking the Almighty for obstacles
in my path, whatever He sees fit to erect will do.

Yesterday a raccoon died on my doorstep,
neck broken, blocking my exit.
I assumed it fell from the balcony,
but this morning I boarded the subway,
the wrong way, ended up in Etobicoke.

Mothers work in mysterious ways.

6. Body Cartographers

Listening a photograph
of my inner landscape.
Ultrasound: matter speaks.

For eons poets
and mystics called crazy for hearing it.
Now, Progress.
        Sound rendered sight rendered
            taste and touch and smell.

Physicians measuring
melting pots of senses.

            The death of trope.

My soul doth magnify the liver,
            all these great-fun gadgets hum.
Sounds, says the medical imagist,
like a spectrum of fatty deposits.
Better cut out the rich desserts.

7. *Valentines*

"Why the liver?" you want to know.
"A kidney would be less painful."

In Shakespeare's time, the liver
was known to possess an array
of qualities since migrated
to an (undeserving, if I might say) heart.

Valour. Romance. Lust.
Poor liver, what has it left

but cancer, ravages of addiction.
Soul consuming itself.

Well, Liver, here it is,
                    Love's moving back in!

No more Valentines shaped like hearts,
unsubtle thumping things.

Skeptical, you ask,
"Are you sure you're not just bitter?"

8. You Complete Me

My liver will live
on in Anonymous,

whom they tell me I must never meet.
The ease of ignorant choice
uncluttered by motivation.

I don't buy it.
I've learned a bit
about this Anonymous:

a prolific artist,
which is no surprise,
having also borne witness
to an extraordinary number of crimes.

Almost certainly adopted.

The twin from whom
I was excised at birth?

I knew it.
That vague feeling of
                                        gap

9. All Out of Proportion

"Are you aware," you ask,
"they'll take sixty percent
of the organ leaving you
less than half?"

I'm not surprised,
the general inequality
          of things being equal

to the disproportionate distribution of luck,

the mortal body being the great equivalizer
          and also
                    not.

It only makes sense.

10. Penitence

You want to see my bank records.
Suspect I am hard up?

You counselled a prisoner once, (manslaughter, several
    assaults),
who traded a kidney for early parole,

convinced you of his ardent, penitent
desire to repay moral debts.

Till he tracked down the organ
recipient, demanded twenty thousand,
                                        cash.

11. I Feel Your Pain

Giving an excised organ, I explain,
is the only scenario
        in which physical (that is real)
discomfort can alleviate
physical (that is legitimate)
        pain in another.

That'll shut them up,
ridiculing the flaky poet,
her dedication to the immaterial.

"I smell a contradiction," you say.
"You can't prove the pen is mightier than the scalpel
by going under the knife."

You are wrong. I might prove to myself
the worth of un-excisable life.
But I turn the table on you and ask
what should my motive be?

Your response is muffled by the thick Formica.

12. Trick with a Knife

Accusation: "You've had no experience
with physical pain."

The table has left a welt on your temple,
as on forcepped newborn.
"You don't know what you're getting into."

That's why we keep coming here.
          Tricked into birth,
sliced into the world
and then it's too late, isn't it?
Scabs of flesh clot up around us.

It always works
for no one
          will be dissuaded

               from the unimaginable.

13. Altruism

The Latin *alteri huic* translates "to this other,"
(the intrinsic value of being
in doubt, but never
the otherness of being).

I will attempt to define altruism as an attempt
        to imagine another's pain.

What I'm really saying is:
        altruism as

            failure of imagination.

The richest man in Georgia
gave a kidney and all of his wealth.
I wish to begin, he said,
to live a moral life.

14. The Privilege of Intellectual Suffering

The hostage's family received irrefutable proof
of his beheading.
(You won't call me liverless, will you,
if I ask the nature of this proof?)

For it gives me no pleasure,
            I want to express

want to say I am
                  it is

Denied their heads and, as such
the capacity for

how to explain, I want
                  not to
                      understand
            I am
not
                      responsible?

Unmendable bridge, (the neck).
Comprehension necessitates physical suffering
which is the loss of comprehension.

So here it is true:
                  understanding is material,
                  being, a moral dilemma.

15. Purgatory

Shed your hair shirt
and dump those peas from your shoes.
Guard against
any sense of insurance
          precluding future pain.

Czeslaw Milosz is dead,
lived to be ninety-three,
which can be regarded as proof
and refutation both, of the necessity
of historical suffering.

When did the thumb of fate ever stop
to calculate the im/moral surplus
of the fleas it squashed?

16. Wormhole

The prayer chain has succeeded
in spreading a virulent worm. Poor Mom.

The Almighty's plan, perhaps, to lure me
through the city, with software to purge
her infected computer,

and right into the trap of a mother's pain

I have failed to imagine.

The inevitability of inflicting suffering on one
in the process of assuaging another's
equals the amorality of love.

Should I take the subway or the streetcar?
What if Anonymous is a serial killer?

17. Out of Body

Prepped, in a hospital bed.
Not prepared – as if one could ever be.
Objectified, no responsibility.
            Floating.

"It's not too late to change your mind,"
you stress.
            Wrong again.
            The un-exorcisability of experience.

Mom was here and left.
Weeping, she asked me to check
whether Jesus was in my heart. I nodded,
            though I'm pretty sure he's in my liver.

You sigh, "Just don't expect to wake
and find the stone rolled away."
            Soft dark caving in,
            I'm rambling, freed of empiricism.

And don't be surprised
by continued
                ordinariness

            Here I go,
            thank you,
            blow me a kiss

Acknowledgements

The author wishes to thank Doug, Nancy, Dan, Jackie, Kimberly, Lindsay and Joey Roorda for their love and support. Thanks also to Molly Peacock for her perspicacity and advice; to Sue Bowness, Sue Chenette, Maureen Scott Harris, Kerri Huffman, Helen Humphreys, Steve Lavender, Ruth Roach Pierson, Patty Rivera and Norma Rowen for many helpful suggestions; and to Antonio D'Alfonso for all his hard work. Some of these poems have appeared in slightly different form in *Arc, The Writing Space Journal, MOBIUS,* and *Hammered Out*.